The sea with no one in it

THE SEA
with no one in it

NIKI KOULOURIS

The Porcupine's Quill

Library and Archives Canada Cataloguing in Publication

Koulouris, Niki, 1965–, author
   The sea with no one in it / Niki Koulouris.

Poems.
ISBN 978-0-88984-363-9 (pbk.)

   1. Ocean—Poetry. I. Title.

PS8621.O94S42 2013   C811'.6   C2013-905847-8

Copyright © Niki Koulouris, 2013.
1   2   3   •   15   14   13

Readied for the press by Kenneth Sherman.

Published by The Porcupine's Quill, 68 Main Street, PO Box 160,
Erin, Ontario N0B 1T0. http://porcupinesquill.ca

All rights reserved. No reproduction without prior written permission of the publisher except brief passages in reviews. Requests for photocopying or other reprographic copying must be directed to Access Copyright.

Represented in Canada by Canadian Manda.
Trade orders are available from University of Toronto Press.

We acknowledge the support of the Ontario Arts Council and the Canada Council for the Arts for our publishing program. The financial support of the Government of Canada through the Canada Book Fund and the Government of Ontario through the Ontario Media Development Corporation is also gratefully acknowledged.

For Markos and Georgia Koulouris

Table of Contents

PART ONE

1. I'm fond of ships 11
2. It looks like the ocean 12
3. Don't mention the sea 13
4. You'll miss more than the road 14
5. You prefer these battles 15
6. When night spiked 16
7. As evening misses 17
8. As you look out 18
9. The closer you look 19
10. If I'm the type 20
11. Today of all days 21
12. Today the fish are sober 22
13. The sea does not need lions 23
14. As for the sea 24
15. Any day you walk the shore 25
16. It was there all along 26
17. The shoreline tells you 27
18. Now the sea has the likeness 28
19. A target at sea level 29
20. World worship at the consulate 30

PART TWO

21. You have given me a city 33
22. So it's lightning 34
23. Arrows for stone fruit/Did I leave the San Franciso Museum 35
24. In a pact with an owl 37
25. The bear is carved 38
26. I write for the beast 39
27. If anything, he kept his onions 40
28. I've come to expect Guernica 41
29. These animals, they keep their heads 43
30. Why think of her as the stranger 44
31. As wide as the foot 45
32. I bought a souvenir of New York 46
33. In a turquoise cab 47
34. You don't have to be finished 48
35. I am aware of It and Lunch 49
36. You may decide 50
37. Where were stars 51
38. The impish drizzle 52
39. The palm trees along the shore 53
40. This is the new office 54
41. These are works barely made 55
42. Admire the forest 56
43. Should I think of the river 57
44. It's always midnight 58

The sea floats its own epigraph.

PART ONE

There are so many waves
it's hard to know where to begin

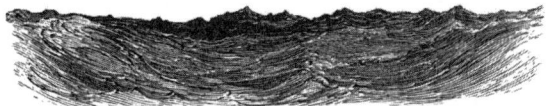

1.

I'm fond of ships
their progress,
the turning weather
for they are never without alternatives
and they may contain the whole population of the mountains
their disasters leave us without suspicion;
leave us stranger

I've seen the ocean once
and I know it has potential
the only way to look at it
is as if it is familiar
there must be more to this than tides,
forgetting language,
neighbourhoods,
the centre of the city;
I want to understand the voyage
these qualms beneath my feet.

2.

It looks like the ocean
with its cargo of gunpowder and ash
bottles the colour of bulls
from another era
longhorns moving ahead
and not much else

once it had been
half man, half sea
unhealed, yet unwounded
by the greyest of steeples

I do not think of the deep
what has been worn
will be worn again by sheiks

why leave these shores
when the rest of the waves
will come to us

what more can they bring us
these waves
with their Formula-One
alligator instincts
but vast zithers
and drop sheets that
fall short of rafts.

3.

Don't mention
the sea
her great hide
for she is perfect
without a shield
a torch
an ending

you can't go on
exactly like this
chanting until
the ocean is complete

for her waves
will never be yours
even if you are not
mistaken

her heart is solid fire
her eyes are weak

if it is not the sea
it is the shores

where would you be
without regrets?

4.

You'll miss more than the road
the opus of June to December
the small riot on the hour

lights up ahead
loose change, too much to ignore,
as the bus blogs on
as a newborn Onassis

it's a sleek formula that makes a path
the long-stemmed wipers arrested
and storage warehouses
sealed prisons that they are

even if It does not arrive in time,
Siemens, IKEA, RusselMetals aside,
It's on its way
as if crossing the Pacific.

5.

for Theseus

You prefer these battles
to anything else
and you must fight abroad
not with your own kind
but with animal will
to prove that you are
who you are
so that there are no
misunderstandings

and when you return
a thorn crossing the Aegean
what matters is not what
you bring with you
or the sails you forgot
to switch back but
that you set out upon
a broad track.

6.

When night spiked
its wingless river
I became freight
until I reached your statue

its spurs propped up
on the shore
among the bolts
and the ruins
and the blonde carnations
and the rams that go to war.

7.

As evening misses,
you'll always believe
in stars and globes and grass
and the trees and the cities and
it's not always easy to watch
the skies, their train wrecks

it's not as if they always come to you, great failures
with their fishbone
of passengers, whale tails, mosques, bright
emus and all.

8.

for Icarus

As you look out
across the Aegean
it will become
the colour of a stork

in awe of the pristine wings
you'll shed like estranged
harlot Siamese sisters
saloon doors to dawn

since you will find
you will be done
with them because,
not wanting you, the sea
never closes
unlike the sun.

9.

The closer you look
the less you'll see
the sleight of luggage labels
from Cairo, Saigon, Capri
among confiscated nudes

I should have gone
through the trash
of St Moritz,
changed course before
the frontline season
of Renaissance flesh,
archived the South-sea hula

but there is no such thing
as folly here,
just used coasters from Hades
and all the stamps in the world
in a resort of footpaths
with more to come.

10.

If I'm the type
to remind you
of the sea
I am an actress

if you can see night
dead in my eyes
you're on a late train
heading for the ocean

missing, yet alive.

11.

Today of all days
this is the sea with no one in it
is this all it will be
unable to dye all it touches
in primitive ink

what could you give the sea
but your stripes,
since you ask,
your war paint, your blindfolds
your appetite for westerns
in exchange for waves
as wide as trains
from the next frontier.

12.

Today the fish are sober
underlined by other fish
actuaries, surgeons, archers
they arrive
in the order of fish

again no one is snorkelling
in these seas
there are so many
waves, it's hard to know
where to begin

in summer there are no
holidays for fish
maybe they take them
in the spring

what better day
to work as watchmen
of three islands
turning to the sixth

and when they die
among the stethoscopes
they'll find these shores
have ribs

still, they must have
recollections
of the steak of Africa,
the broken comma
of New Zealand.

13.

The sea does not need lions in it
needless elephants and bears
from here there is nothing to behold
but the solitary cranking out of waves
though speared it has no enemies
it does not need ashes in it
seldom crosses
in some cases casks

the sea does not need 4711
eau de cologne in it
certainly no Brylcreem
all of Alabama or the NYPD
and I am sure the sea does
not need Jack Kerouac
to take a stab at it

the sea can do without gondolas
there are few gondolas in the sea
and you'll find enough stoushes
without straits full of sceptres

but most of all the sea does not need
the bestriped in it
only one or more ships
and contraband
for the midway sea.

14.

As for the sea
it has no number, no colour
though it's been illustrated
I can understand how it looks
to a porcupine on the high road
or three new-world owls in the trees

realmless bridge, here
while there, irresolute flag
of those who know
the whereabouts of the cowled
who walked on sand
as dangerous as bread.

15.

Any day you walk the shore
there will be waves in the ocean
and there will be no mistaking
all the sails you will see
yet this is not all you will find
now the land is full of miscreants
on unfamiliar horses

it seems you have thought of every fish
for a moment, every prow
knowing that elsewhere there are lions
loyal to the ground, gathered there
where scouts have been

remind me of tournaments
now we have sailed
remind me of wide parades
watched by the denizens
of the wildest ravines.

16.

It was there all along
as if undiscovered
the modern sea
already alive, sawn off
craved by gravel
summoned by the populace
that salvaged pendants
from the surgery of tides

even though it was the sea
it did not seem like it
nor did it seem like what it could be
it was not the sea I missed
on its way to another age

it has always been like the sky
on a day no one is born
it has become its counterpart
a half icon, as permanent,
from where can it be seized
how should it be adorned?

17.

The shoreline tells you to
walk no farther than these men
today all the more Melbournian, barbarian

do they recognize each other
standing in TV snow
all the same height
as if in a Peter Booth drawing
or treading water
or treading water in a Peter Booth drawing
their flesh of undone bandages, boughs
that at daybreak strap-dangled
branches fetched
by swallows
from the undertow of cables

commuters with the foreknowledge
of dawn and the coming of Stelarc
in from the league of waves
looking for their tunics
underfoot.

Peter Booth: born 1940, Australian surrealist painter.

Stelarc: Australian performance artist and elder of public bodily suspensions.

18.

Now the sea has the likeness
of the waves and the waves
have the likeness of the sea
even when it's dark
it is still called the sea

you look at it as if it
were not always there
it is almost always there
always almost there
it will arrive
in the year of the train

when I think of the sea
it is never like this
look at it as if it
is all you will see

it is here because
you thought of it
and because you thought of it
it is dynamite

how is it it will
always be where
you were.

19.

A target at sea level
is yellow, red, blue and white
the four colours left in the world—
the one that does not turn
in front of you
or in any forest
as round as its boiled-bright yolk
is its sombre penultimate halo
still as a flat planet, inept cog
Mod mainspring, stopped master clock

throw no stones
why wouldn't you slug it from afar
with its very own hands
mark your own time,
the odd hours you keep,
by their narrow accusatorial shadows.

20.

World worship at the consulate of Jasper Johns

When this was a flag in a shoreless sky
all fields were states
or parts of the sea themselves
the sea of identical parts
and this was a rectangle
before these were overused numbers

when this was the sea there were
as many stars
in the fields as these targets—
each one the roundest of fruit
that was halved

you can't miss the sky
you can't miss the sea, the full-length
numbers that dye absent mountains,
perhaps the un-numbered stars

what has become of the sky outnumbered by stars
what has become of the ocean outnumbered by waves

when this was a star, this was a shield
and this was a helmet
and this is a flag
for an uncrossed sky.

PART TWO

I've come to expect Guernica

21.

for Anselm Kiefer

You have given me
a city without buildings
in a cold republic
all roads lie where they fell

now even night
would not surprise me
an airlift of shells

I will prove
you have painted Nero's ocean,
or a landscape razed for battle
in a season without opposite

we can lose track forever
of a wave in the ocean
once yoked by planes
that fly as low as yesterday

no doubt
it needed ripe pineapples
this staid riviera,
and red-figure crustaceans
shot down from the sky.

22.

So it's lightning that herds
them nightly to this place
headstones,
waves unanimous in death,
enscale the buried
for whom all hours tighten
their alpenstock grip
and hold up like rain
its ankle braces reeling
like the haloes of vermin
the hooves they took
for telephones
or the zeros in a
zillion.

23.

ARROWS FOR STONE FRUIT

for Philip Guston

1.

Did I leave the San Francisco
Museum of Modern Art terrified of lemons,
when I imagined the artist as a boy of ten,
standing there alone, at the local grocer's, looking up
at suspended scales loaded with fruit? Had his errand pre-
empted the afternoon piece of pie he was taking his father,
pie that stained his hands magenta as he tilted its plate
when wrenching open, somehow with small fingers,
the door to the shed?

2.

I remember being menaced by a still life that day
that flamingo-abattoir off-pink hit-and-run double-decker
of a bus, by Philip Guston, born in Montreal, moved to
California, finished up in Woodstock, New York,
painter of cartoon Klansmen, distended bricks, light bulbs,
an eye or two, paintbrushes, the under soles of boots,
the odd telephone and sandwich, plank, clock
and cigarette rolled into a snail,
a man de-plenishing his cornucopia of jetsam,
by depicting its contents, as if fruit never existed,
except for a few pounds of cherries punctured
by their own stems.

3.

Do you really want to see shoe soles
on a table a few feet away from a cigarette
that's burning its way to the table's edge
or a grazed one-eyed kidney bean
read *Memoirs of the Damned*
or almost mount a bottle of Beaujolais?

maybe a portrait of the artist in bed
smoking, eating, painting with
singed brushes dipped in rosewater
that smells of sardines

or a landscape painted with cold
pig trotters or an unravelled
wire coat hanger dipped in Valvoline

a besieged knoll of cherries,
a sunburnt Ku Klux Klan carpool

now that all that is pink
in the world is alive
you never know when you will.

24.

for Jackson Pollock

In a pact with an owl
you wade through
the cramped reflections of a lake
so many nights on short fuse wire
you drive like a gelding

through fog
through headlights
those two canoes
lifted like sleepers
in a dark parade.

25.

(Logic deployed while comparing a Kwakiutl First Nation
wooden wall carving of a bear to that of an eagle at an aboriginal
art shop on Granville Island Vancouver, B.C.)

The bear is carved
by the same man
as the eagle

both painted the red and green
of 1940s rose bushes, law books,
telephones

it is true no man
carved out the owl-eyed phone
and maybe if he had
he would have had until it rang
to finish his mask of kings

the carver perceived as a threat
by his creation's pop-up horns,
as he answered the call of the wild
made without beak or maw or dialled
for pizza without claw or paw.

26.

for Maurice Sendak

I write for the beast
about how late it is for company
I will deliver even night;
the book itself.

I've lost molecules to
feudal, untroubled
monsters

are these my parents
swinging from the trees?

I take the world to heart
in my paper hat
for I am the only wolf I know

my feet are lilies
I occupy my conception
I will not die motherless, fatherless
supper less.

27.

for Cézanne

If anything
he must have kept his onions
in a safe
but I think of Cézanne's apples,
peaches, pears
turning like
doorknobs
in a house full of
surprises

restless fruit
tuned at high noon
by the grocer's scales

oranges on togas
on tables,
still-blooded, spared.

28.

I've come to expect
Guernica on the
street

ask me why I wake up
I'll tell you nothing

to my surprise
there were wares
outside

smoke awnings
a face or two
shovelled east

arms or barracuda
boilerplate flowers
jazz hands

you published *that*
instead of this?

there can be only
seven days a week

well or alive
I took it upon
myself to check

a formidable horse
drinks from tinted water
strikes oil

the band is
paid to screech

this has to be
a pair of skis

a typewriter
(just played)
before lunch

on its knees.

29.

for the aurochs, dragons and lions
of the restored Ishtar Gates in Berlin's Pergamon Museum

These animals
they keep their heads
on a path without
distractions

far from venatores, saints
and delicatessens
re-unified
they are Berliners
free to walk
among the highest stalks
the brightest gods
a city wall their track.

30.

for the Chian Kore, c. 510 B.C. in the Acropolis Museum

Why think of her as the stranger
she has become—
her crown has no star
nor does she reach for
the sky, the sword,
a tassel

her right forearm
a severed tusk
taken with what
she is
offering.

31.

As wide as the foot
of this bed
it looks to me
like Cleopatra's bier
or cuneiform

you will wonder
about the ironing board
cut from stone wall
and vintage iron
for as long as you live.

32.

I bought a souvenir
of New York
in San Francisco

I'm not immune
to bringing home
world fixtures

be wary of all things
smaller than they are
or bigger than they seem

sphinxes such as these
appear more tanned,
more invincible
in snow domes
than they've ever been.

33.

In a turquoise cab
on the way from O'Hare Airport
behind a cement mixer convoy,
it occurs to me the world's no
Chicago Illinois—
birthplace of Walt Disney
the malted milkshake
pinball machine, window
envelope and Twinkie
with more Nobel laureates
per hectare than anywhere—
These are Chicago's secrets
confides Taxi TV (who squealed?)
don't worry, Mayor R.M. Daley,
these lips are sealed.

34.

You don't have to be finished
to know
you've gone to the dogs
there's a point
at which we're all doomed,
one way or
another,
and you know it's
the days that count
or else the
misadventures,
once and for all,
yet, you never
expected the
end to
bite so
soon.

35.

I am aware of It and Lunch
of life and the baby
that could appear somewhere between
the 31st and the 1st

but does it matter
who I am
to a cosmonaut
as I write this:
Lunch is a fix;
life plays its tricks
and no one is naked
here for long.

36.

You may decide
watching rain is like
watching a foreign movie
with foreign subtitles

soon it will leave
rivets in ivy
thin nations on windscreens
the holes of centimes
or drachmas,
the diameters of drams
the radii of shillings
and the axes of strawberries
on glass

its Shaker style
in windows
as you cross
some isthmus,
as a life-size
marionette

convinced they do not seem like much—
the sceptres of flowers
you saw because it has rained.

37.

Where were stars before Rome
another Rome
and who are these tourists looking
at Michelangelo's David
as if he were an undressed skin diver
in a glass elevator held up
for some reason on the second floor

therein holding his slingshot over his shoulder
his shins like the undersides of twin sharks
bare feet yet to defy the minefields of a modern city
or walk over star-deep linoleum
to meet the shallow-wristed tide
from where he might consider hurling
that stone into the water.

38.

The impish drizzle draws
its trombone rail; curious
and shoulder-steep
it laps at its epaulette straps

in pale balloons the snails approach
no shelter from these shards;
from fabled worlds dense ground
withholds the gamut of the stars.

39.

Meditations from St Kilda's Esplanade Hotel, Melbourne

The palm trees along the shore
outlived the stars—
afternoon's Alpine-cigarette-lit rinks—
and the bongos too must go on
played by offspring of the dead
and so must the whale go on
without a fable
there are few places left
like this for the doomed to drink
beneath bygone clouds of
Lolly Gobble Bliss Bomb bliss
so the sea's not for everyone
you can see why from here
from the steps of the Esplanade
under a slab portico fifty hands high
wide as the wingspan of Pegasus.

Lolly Gobble Bliss Bombs—Australian version of the Cracker Jack popular in the 1970s.

40.

Ornettology on Broadway and 15th, Oakland CA
after a 460 degree rotation at 8th

This is the new office of the stars
black like a bare American widow
in the tombless darkness
there may be an exit

black like a bare American widow
the river is a swing
wide as the waist of a snake
very close to land

very close to landing
the river is a swing
for heretical stars
jammed in the sky

heretical stars
shieldless as this realm
low key as pyramids
awakened without music

shieldless as this realm
awakened without music
the target's a brooch I wear
between Trappist jungles

in the tombless darkness
black like a bare American widow
there may be an exit
wide as the waist of a snake.

41.

for Cy Twombly

These are works barely made
in a time to plant odd numbers
at least there was rubble in the meadow

I may have thought of the sea myself
fenced off by Roman numerals
while working back at night

is it the nearly-deep Mediterranean
of cold helmets and low wonky pagodas
of the late late 1950s

biding my time
I exhumed funnels, rungs
touched up cenotaphs with house paint

concocted gradients (for gurneys)
that never necessarily
wilted

I can hardly know
if I am following protocol
on castors

till I start unbundling
Pan flutes, making opponents
of four fancy origami lungs.

42.

Poem for Gaspésie

Admire the forest as you would the sea
admire a wave among waves
as you would a cross among crosses
but beware the desert—
stars forage here
dragging hammers, axes,
sceptres.

43.

Should I think of the river at night
as a city burns its brow
the river that is no longer metal
at night I will think of the bridge

as a city burns its brow
on a night of a thousand renegades
at night I will think of the bridge
as a blade that might turn a fly to ash

on a night of a thousand renegades
admire each underpass star
each fly that lands on a blade
by then it will exist this river

admire each underpass star
tell me that it's wise to smoke in church
by then it will exist this river
of fuselage and unbound crosses

tell me that it's wise to smoke in church
write convent graffiti
at night I will think of the bridge
of fuselage and unbound crosses

on a night of a thousand renegades
as a city burns its brow
by then it will exist this river
should I think of the river at night?

44.

It's always midnight
in the river
between two poems

the river
no wider than
a cross

no longer
than the journey

you are a fish
in the Seine

the midnight mast
of the brakeless
Nile

camped like
the spire
of this book.

Acknowledgements

'When night spiked' and 'In a pact with an owl' were published in *The Cortland Review* Poetry Issue 38, February 2008.

Thanks to Kenneth Sherman, Tim and Elke Inkster, David Donnell, Ginger Murchison, Judith Rodriguez, Carleton Wilson, Kathleen Icely, Michael Fraser (Plasticene Poetry Series), James Dewar (Hot Sauced Words), Rob Welch/Art Bar Team (Art Bar Poetry), Stephanie Small, Sharolyn Vettese, Doris Cowan, Philip Heiland, C. David Weyman, Judy Tate, Lynne Boutette, Rita Wilder-Craig and David Redgrave.

About the Poet

Niki Koulouris was born in Melbourne, Australia, and is a graduate of the University of Melbourne and RMIT University. She has worked as a staff writer and editor at Victoria University. Her poetry and prose have appeared in *The Cortland Review, Space, Subtext Magazine* and *The Age*. A beer enthusiast, she has been known to start spontaneous lists on napkins of her top India Pale Ales. Niki lives in Toronto.